W9-AWR-167

A PICTURE BOOK OF
ISRAEL

A Sabra
CONSULATE GENERAL OF ISRAEL

A PICTURE BOOK OF
ISRAEL

David A. Adler

HOLIDAY HOUSE/NEW YORK

to my brother Eddie,
in loving memory

The author wishes to thank Chaya M. Burstein for providing the map on page 8 and the following who helped by providing the photographs: Edward M. Adler, Nathan Adler, Carol Sue Davidson, the New York office of the Consulate General of Israel, the Israel Government Tourist Office and the Zionist Archives.

Library of Congress Cataloging in Publication Data

Adler, David A.
  A picture book of Israel.

  Includes index.
  1. Israel—Description and travel—Views—Juvenile literature. I. Title.
DS107.4.A22 1984   915.694′0022′2   83-18613
ISBN 0-8234-0513-3

The remains of an ancient synagogue in
Capernaum, a village in northern Israel
ISRAEL GOVERNMENT TOURIST OFFICE

Modern Jerusalem
CONSULATE GENERAL OF ISRAEL

Israel is an old country with a history that stretches back
thousands of years, to the time of the Bible. And it's a new
country with new methods of farming, modern buildings,
factories and research centers.

CONSULATE GENERAL OF ISRAEL   DAVID A. ADLER

Israel is a holy land for Jews, Christians and Moslems.
Israel is a land of students, workers, soldiers, scholars and children.

The Mediterranean Sea
DAVID A. ADLER

Israel lies between the Mediterranean Sea and the Arab countries of Egypt, Jordan, Syria and Lebanon. In summer Israel is a hot, dry country. In winter Israel is cooler and it rains. Almost all of Israel's rain falls between November and March, Israel's "rainy season."

Throughout the year wildflowers bloom on hillsides and in valleys. Fig, orange, pomegranate and date-palm trees grow in Israel.

Old olive trees in northern Israel

And there are a great many olive trees, some one thousand years old, which blossom every summer and bear fruit in the early fall.

About half of Israel is desert, sand and rocks baking under a burning sun. Israel's desert is called the "Negev."

At the edge of the Negev is the lowest spot on Earth, the Dead Sea. It's a big, unmoving body of water which is loaded with salt and other minerals. The Dead Sea is so salty that nothing, not even the smallest fish or piece of seaweed, can live in it.

Crystallized salt at the edge of the Dead Sea
ISRAEL GOVERNMENT TOURIST OFFICE

CONSULATE GENERAL OF ISRAEL

Beersheba, the largest city in the Negev, got its name about four thousand years ago when Abraham, the father of the Jewish people, and a local king dug a well as a sign of their treaty of peace. Beersheba means "well of promise." Today it's a modern city with large factories, colleges and research centers.

Beersheba is a market center for the Bedouin Arabs living in the Negev. Many live in modern apartments in Beersheba. Others still live in the desert, in goatskin tents. They move their tents from one place to another in search of water and grass for their sheep and goats.

Bedouin goatskin tents, some covered with brush
CONSULATE GENERAL OF ISRAEL

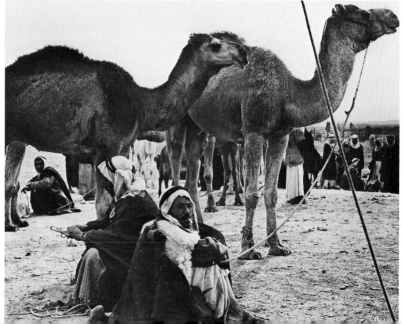

Bedouins in Beersheba on market day
CONSULATE GENERAL OF ISRAEL

A scuba diver in the Red Sea,
off the coast of Eilat

At the southern tip of the Negev is Eilat, a hot resort city with beautiful beaches and the clear water of the Red Sea.

Through glass-bottom boats, tourists watch schools of
small, colorful fish swim among beautiful coral formations.

Fish among the coral

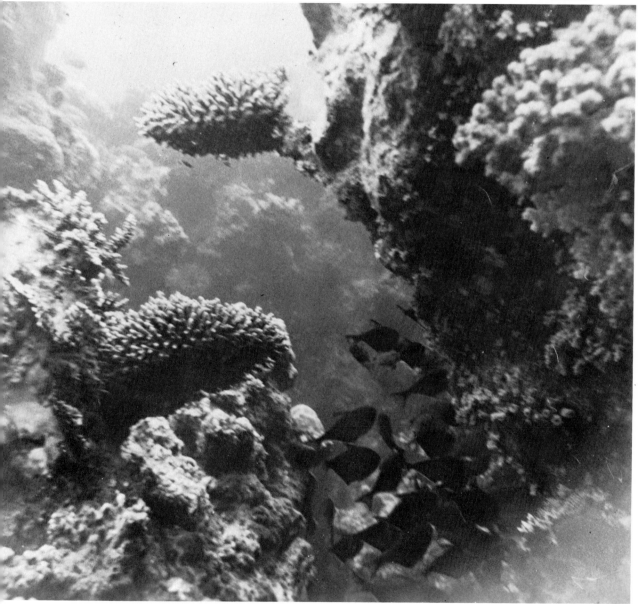

Haifa and Safed are cities in northern Israel. Haifa is built on a mountain, Mount Carmel. At its base is Haifa harbor, crowded with navy and cargo ships and fishing boats.

Old Jerusalem in the eastern half of the city is surrounded by a high stone wall hundreds of years old.

EDWARD M. ADLER

There are narrow, winding, cobblestone lanes inside the wall, lined with dark shops selling pottery, souvenirs, fruits, vegetables, breads and Arab pastries.

New Jerusalem is a modern city with factories, hotels and the Knesset building, where Israel's government meets. All citizens over eighteen, men and women, Arabs and Jews, Christians and Moslems can vote to elect the one-hundred-and-twenty members of the Knesset who govern Israel.

The Knesset building
ISRAEL GOVERNMENT TOURIST OFFICE

Throughout the cities of Israel there are reminders of her past.

Rachel's Tomb is in Bethlehem. Rachel was Jacob's wife. She lived almost four thousand years ago and was one of the "Four Mothers of Israel."

Close to Jerusalem is the Elah Valley where David slew Goliath. And in the middle of Jerusalem, in the Old City, is the "Wailing Wall," the western section of the outer wall which surrounded the Second Temple. The Second Temple was destroyed by the Romans almost two thousand years ago. The First Temple which stood on the same site, was destroyed by the Babylonians some five hundred years earlier.

The "Wailing Wall"
ISRAEL GOVERNMENT TOURIST OFFICE

Near the Dead Sea is another reminder of the Romans. There, on top of a huge, flat rock is an ancient fortress, Masada. At Masada one thousand Jews held off a Roman army for three years, until the Romans were about to break through. Then the Jews took their own lives rather than be taken by the enemy.

Over the next almost two thousand years there were numerous battles and sieges and the land passed from the Romans to the Moslems, Christian Crusaders, Turks and then to the British.

A Crusader fortress many hundreds of years old still stands in Caesarea. And the walls which surround Old Jerusalem were built by the Turks some four hundred years ago.

The theater at Caesarea built two thousand years ago by the Jewish king Herod
CAROL SUE DAVIDSON

Throughout Israel there are walls with bullet holes in them. And on the sides of roads, there are the remains of tanks. These are reminders of Israel's wars with the surrounding Arab countries. Israel's first war was in 1948, when she became a state. It was her War of Independence, her War of Liberation. As soon as the state was declared, five Arab states attacked. But Israel survived. There have been other attacks and other wars with her neighboring Arab countries, and there are many statues—memorials to the soldiers who died defending the land.

Yad Vashem in Jerusalem

CONSULATE GENERAL OF ISRAEL

Throughout Israel there are also reminders of her more recent history.

During the Second World War millions of innocent Jews in Europe were murdered by the German Nazis. Many Jews trying to escape had nowhere to go. Even the land that would one day be Israel was almost completely closed to them. Its borders were guarded to keep the Jews out. Today, in Jerusalem, there's a memorial to those killed by the Nazis. It's called Yad Vashem.

Monument to the Israeli airmen who died
during Israel's War of Liberation
ZIONIST ARCHIVES

Monument to the fighters who died
defending the road to Jerusalem
in the War of Liberation
CONSULATE GENERAL OF ISRAEL

A street sign in Old Jerusalem
ISRAEL GOVERNMENT TOURIST OFFICE

The official language of Israel is Hebrew, the language of the Bible. But because the people of Israel have such a variety of backgrounds, the writing on Israeli money—the shekel—and on Israeli stamps is often written in three languages—Hebrew, Arabic and English. Even some signs are written in all three languages.

Israel is a Jewish country, but not all its people are Jews. There is a large Arab community in Israel. Many Arabs have lived there for generations. Many more Arabs came under Israeli rule after the 1967 war, when Israel gained control over additional land, including the Old City of Jerusalem.

A Bedouin Arab
CONSULATE GENERAL OF ISRAEL

An Arab schoolgirl
CONSULATE GENERAL OF ISRAEL

Two girls studying in an Arab school
CONSULATE GENERAL OF ISRAEL

Most of the Arabs in Israel are Moslems. Throughout Israel there are mosques—Moslem churches—with large domes and tall minarets. Five times a day *muezzins*, servants of the mosques, stand on the balconies of the minarets and call their people to prayer.

There are also Christian Arabs. Many of them live in Nazareth, Bethlehem and Jerusalem.

Mosque of Al Aksa in Jerusalem
ISRAEL GOVERNMENT TOURIST OFFICE